The Gift of Grief
Poems
by
T. L. Cooper

Copyright © 2024 T. L. Cooper
All rights reserved. Published in the United States by The TLC Press.

ISBN-13: 978-1-943736-06-5

DEDICATION

For those who've taught me that to grieve is to recognize the gift of knowing you. The list is long and many of these poems were written with you in mind. For those who have grieved with me in silence or out loud as we shared the gift grief brings us in our memories. For those who need to feel less alone in their grief journey as you discover your loved ones live on in your memories making your grief feel like a gift of connection.

Bubbly Memories

Dipping my sorrow
Into this well of joy
Feeling your memory
Bubble around me
Like ice cold champagne
Sparking light in the effervescence
Of the love you lived
The cold crystal glass
Trapping the moments
I can't remember as the ones
I can't forget break the surface
All those moments living in suspension
Of the reality of your absence
Even as my pain dips into the pleasure
Of every sip of every memory
Tickling my heart and mind
With the intoxication of denial
Of the grief that lingers on my tongue
And burns the back of my throat
Like the first drink of bourbon

Celebrate Life

As we see mourn our loss
Let us remember our gain
For a soul to have touched us so deeply
Gratitude for your life fills my heart
As I focus on the inspiration you remain
Your life was never lived in vain
You offered the world so much
Now it is up to us to take the torch
March on toward unity and peace
In your words, in your heart, in your life
You showed us the meaning of strength
You taught us the power of perseverance
You gave us the joy of your smile
You reminded us all
We are here to serve one another
We have a responsibility to live the change we seek
So I lift my voice in celebration of a life purposefully lived
Even as my eyes tear with sadness at the world's loss

Forever a Memory

You're now only a memory
I never expected that to happen
We shared so much
I thought you'd stay beside me
I thought we'd build a future
I thought we'd create memories together
Forever
Forever seemed so possible
On those days when we laughed
Even on the days when we cried
We never considered a day
When all that would be left would be a memory
Yet it seems that day has come
Far sooner than forever
And yet I do believe it will last forever
You're not and forevermore only a memory

One I Remember

You're the one I remember
When my heart forgets
Who I am
Deep in that place
Where the light hides from shadows
You're the one I remember
When the blooms dry up on the azalea bush
Clinging to their base with all their might
Turning from red to a dull dark brown
Sadness in the midst of greenery
You're the one I remember
When the snow melts
Leaving puddles of muddy water
Across my path
Filled with rotting leaves
You're the one I remember
When the summer sun scorches
The ground leaving cracks where tears fall unbidden
My heart aches and struggles to find
The joy in my journey
Because every time I remember you
I forget who I am

Summit

I lost you
Somewhere where the air thinned
Where the sun reflected off the snow
And the trees turned into boulders
Sitting in a dry oasis
Muddy water roaring below
I looked into the past
Saw you fading away
Toward a horizon
Too far away to reach
Lost the moment
When our connection
Tethered us to a future
Standing on that mountain
Surveying my journey
The trail behind me littered
With regrets of moments that never happened
Fear oozing between those moments
Like so much dust on a forgotten dream
I stood and screamed into the mountain
A volcano of pain released from my mouth
I looked right
I glanced left
I turned my eyes up
I stared down
All around me
The Earth shifting silently under my feet
The wind swaying my body
Changing and staying the same
Destruction and rebirth mingled
In dying trees and seeds dropping
New growth obscuring the danger

Life engorged with uncertainty
In a world that preaches such absolutism
Mountains and valleys
Life and death
Love and hate
No, not hate, loss
Loss is so much harder than hate
Regret holds my hand and walks me slowly
Toward an abandoned heart
Standing strong on the edge of a mountain
See me here
Stepping over the summit
Away from you

Note: Also appeared on YouTube

Strong Absence

Your absence is stronger
Than your presence ever was
When I close my eyes at night
The twinkle in your eyes gleams
One last time
Your smile invites me to kiss your lips
One last time
Your arms reach out to embrace me
One last time
Your breath brushes across my skin
One last time
Your fingers brand me with your feathery touch
One last time
Your heat warms my heart
One last time
Your passion presses against me
One last time
Your words tickle my ear
One last time
Your sigh lingers against my neck
One last time
Your soul meets mine
One last time
And then I realize
Your presence never felt this strong
As I open my eyes
And feel the strength of your absence
One last time

Cloudy Absence

Cloudy skies above
Remind me of your absence
My tears fall like rain

Tritina of Grief

Falling on your steel tears
Wishing for the quiet grace
To bring your heart to peace

Resting in a world lacking peace
Where no one appreciates your tears
As you forego any sense of grace

Admiring the simple art of grace
Living in the heart that's found peace
Through the cleansing power of tears

Tears shed symbolize the peace you brought with grace

Winter Lasts Forever

Sometimes winter seems to last forever
The air smells so cold it hurts
What does cold even smell like?
The cold burns the skin
Icicles falling sound like wind chimes
Until they melt into oblivion
Looking at snow falling from the sky
Clouds of snow billowing on the ground
Tongues out to taste the flakes
Falling from the matching clouds in the sky
The words I heard spoken frozen
Like so much ice in winter
A blizzard of heartache
Burying us all
Making us wonder
If spring will ever release us
From this winter wind
That keeps blowing through our life

Your Smile Floats Through My Dreams

Your smile floats through my dreams
Leaving me reluctant to open my eyes
When the morning sun peeks through the window
Rousing me to another day without you

When the morning sun peeks through the window
I stretch and reach for something I can't touch
Your smile floats through my dreams
Yesterday lives forever in my heart

Rousing me to another day without you
When you left, it felt like my heart would never mend
Leaving me reluctant to open my eyes
Where I had to face life without you

Yesterday lives forever in my heart
A quiet kiss landing on my forehead in a dark room
I stretch and reach for something I can't touch
As the sun sets on another day without you

Where I had to face life without you
I traveled to the ends of the Earth to escape the pain
When you left, it felt like my heart would never mend
Yet here I am facing midnight with a smile on face

As the sun sets on another day without you
I traveled to the ends of the Earth to escape the pain
A quiet kiss landing on my forehead in a dark room

Yet here I am facing midnight with a smile on my face
Your smile floats through my dreams

Morning Wake-Up

The sun rose over my head
Obscured by the clouds of mourning
I couldn't feel the heat
As my tears rained down
The morning dew
Glistening off blades of uncut grass
My heart breaking with the loss
Not quite here
But on the horizon
Another day bought and sold
In an economy of life and love
Future and past
Memories and plans
All rising with the sun
To hold my hand
As I try to avoid
Seeing the day
When the setting sun
Will bring the mourning
Flirting at the edges of my
Every sunrise…

Changing Your Health

Standing by your side
Watching your health fade away
Offering tips and tricks
Anything to keep you here
Just a bit longer
Whatever it takes
Sitting for hours by your side
Wishing for your good health to return
Waiting for the moment that can't come
I looked in the mirror morning after morning
Seeing my own health
Hidden below my grief at the loss of yours
And cursed the world for taking your health
Questioned the methods to save you
Because no matter how hard we tried
To restore your health
It faded
Day by day
Hour by hour
Minute by minute
And there was nothing I could do
I wanted to fix it for you
But you looked in my eyes and begged me
To understand as much as I wanted to
I didn't have the power to change your health
No matter how hard I wished I could
All that was left was to let you be
To let you enjoy what you had left
To let you know I loved you
To hold you close in my heart
To let you go

Reach My Heart

The Earth swallowed you
I watched you slide beyond reach
Your roots held my heart

Under the Shady Oak

I remember the shady oak
Standing tall on the creek bank
A picnic table and stone grill underneath
Daddy standing over the grill he built
Spatula in hand
Staring across the road
Standing back wondering
What he was thinking in that moment
His face impossible to read
I like to think he felt happy
Grilling for the family
While my sister and I
Ran around the yard
With the dogs and cats
A happy moment in a
Life of hard work
Seeing him sigh
His shoulders drop just a bit
Relaxation or exhaustion or capitulation
I've never known
But he turned and smiled when he saw me
And that smile I'll remember forever
Him standing in the dappled shade of that tree
His family, his farm, his life
Surrounding him
And his smile lighting up his face
In what I remember as pure joy
And maybe just maybe
A touch of pride in all
He'd accomplished
A humble man he'd never
Admit that pride

T. L. Cooper

But he deserved to feel it
Standing under that shady oak
In the middle of a life well-lived

Some Endings are Just Endings

Sometimes an ending is just an ending
Nothing drove this home like watching
The light disappear from your eyes
Seeing you lifeless and still
My heart screamed
This is an ending without a beginning
There's no starting over
When you're no longer here
One last look
One last touch
One last tear
Knowing you're never coming back
Couldn't if you wanted to
All the memories I hold in my heart
Aren't you
They aren't beginnings or endings
They are the moments we shared
Living inside me
Reminding me that sometimes
An ending is just an ending

Picking Pink Flowers

Tobacco plants
Taller than my head
Serve as a shade
From the hot sun
The pink blooms
Pretty against the blue sky
As I pluck one and then the next
Smell it and wonder how
Something so pretty smells so foul
I lick my lips
Tasting sweat, tobacco, and sunscreen
Nearing the end of the row
I hear the creek gurgling
You're standing there
That encouraging smile on your face
Though I'm certain I detect a bit of impatience
Or maybe that's more my fear
Because you never said it
The plants also over your head
I pause to pull one of the leaves wide
And realize I can hide behind it
The crop this year will be good
These plants are money in the bank
Food on the table
School clothes
Vacations in summer
I look at my sticky, sore hands
As I reach you at the end
You let me finish the row
All by myself because
You always knew I needed to
Finish the job myself

The Gift of Grief

Just like you
As we walk toward the house together
I look back and see the day's work
You, of course, did so much more than me
You always did
And suddenly I remember you lifting me
To your shoulder and letting me
"Pick the flowers" when I was too small
To do the work
I hated picking those flowers when it became work
But I'd give just about anything to have
One more day with you
Even if it was in the tobacco field
Picking the flowers off tobacco plants
And ending the day with sore, sticky hands
Exhausted beyond belief
To see that look in your eye as you watched me
Finish my row all by myself
Pink flowers littering the ground, trampled and ugly
The field fades away
You fade away
I fade way
Forgotten like those pretty pink flowers

Obscured Grief

We stood under an obscured moon
Our hearts eclipsed with grief
Waiting endlessly for the sun to relieve our loss

Cry for You

I shall cry for you today
Not yesterday or tomorrow
But today I shall let that tear
Travel down my cheek unabated
I'll welcome the salt drying on my skin
And the taste of what could've been
Teasing my lips

I shall cry for you today
Not yesterday or tomorrow
But today I shall let sobs wrack by body
Shake me to my core
I'll welcome the shakes and shivers
And the smell of dreams deserted
Teasing my nostrils

I shall cry for you today
Not yesterday or tomorrow
But today I shall let the pain wash over me
Drown me in sorrow
I'll welcome the foggy mind
And the sound of memories distorted
Teasing my ears

I shall cry for you today
Not yesterday or tomorrow
But today I shall let the loss permeate my shell
Steal into my pores
I'll welcome the goosebumps on my skin
And the caress of what never was
Teasing my skin

I shall cry for you today
Not yesterday or tomorrow
But today I shall let your absence settle around me

Embrace me with sadness
I'll welcome the image of yesterday
And the sight of tomorrow erased
Teasing my eyes

Oh, yes
I shall cry for you today
Not yesterday or tomorrow
But today I'll welcome
The blurred vision
The runny nose
The salty tears
The missing sound
The tightness of chest
The grief of loss
The recognition of pain
The piercing of my heart
To fill the space between
Yesterday and tomorrow

Counting Down the Hours

Counting down the hours
As if there's magic waiting
In that appointed time
When something will change
Even if nothing else does
When everything feels so broken
All we can do is hope that
Anything is better than the moment
So we glance at the clock
Has another hour passed yet
Are we any closer to that magic time
When the world just might feel
A little less shattered and scattered
I hold out for that moment
I don't want to miss it
Just in case that tick of the clock
Really will magically move us
To a better place
Where we can find what we lost
When we turned the world upside down
On a whim
Has another hour passed yet
And will we beg for time to slow down
Once we've finally found the magic hour
We long for

Days Without You

As I look forward I see
Days and days without you
Morphing into
Years and years without you
Never again to see your smile
Never again to hear your voice
Never again to feel your touch
My future without you
Looms before me making me realize
Just how lucky I was to have you
For the time I did
My heart aches
To hold onto each moment we shared
To never forget a single smile
To never forget hearing you speak
To never forget your hand on my arm
But you cannot be there, not any more
So I reach into my heart and my mind
Where you'll live until I take my last breath
Because you are imprinted there

Creek

Holding my small hand
Crossing the turbulent creek
You never dropped me

Take Me

My heart screamed
Take me with you
In the moment you
Let go of your last breath
I wanted to hold your hand
One last time
I wanted to feel your touch
On my arm
One last time
I wanted to go with you
Just like your eyes said
Take me with you
Every time I left
And now you can't come back
And I feel like I'm all alone
Whispering to an empty sky
Take me with you
Until I hear the words
Don't leave me
Behind me
And turn to see
Why I can't let you
Take me with you
No matter how much I miss you

No Savior

There was no saving you
I was no savior
Not for anyone
Least of all you
No matter how hard I tried
Saving you wasn't an option
I listed all the options
And searched for new ones
Even as I knew the option
Just didn't exist
Not in this timeline
Not in this space
Not in this world
But still I couldn't stop trying
Right up until the last minute
Because I knew you were so busy
Trying to save both you and me
From the pain of not being able to
Save you from the inevitable
And still I curse the sky
I scream at the stars
I weep at the sun
Because you deserved to be
Saved
But I failed
Because some things really are impossible
No matter how hard I tried
I am no savior
And I could find no savior

Sorrow

I didn't expect the news
Or my reaction
I read the words
And felt my joy drain
Sorrow slid into its place
We'd reconnected
But not
We'd talked
But not
We'd tried
So many times
But let our schedules interfere
We weren't as close
As we could've been
But I saw in you
A need for family
A desire for simplicity
A longing for connection
A drive to keep trying to be your best self
That I so often feel myself
As the news settled in my heart
I slipped away
Let my tears fall
And wondered
Why we weren't that close
As children
Now you're gone
Just when I felt
We were becoming friends

Under a Pile of Leaves

As the leaves piled
Outside my window
Under the tree
My grief drifted away
On the wind
Leaving me with hope
For a new beginning
As leaves rotted
Disappearing into the ground
My dreams reappeared from
Their hiding place
Under a pile of leaves

Ten Times Ten Times Ten

I looked up at the night sky
Blinked back ten tears
Or maybe one hundred tears
Or maybe one thousand tears.
Who knows?
I refused to let them begin
For fear they'd never end.
I counted the stars above me
Starting over every time I lost my place
Knowing even if I counted by tens
I'd never count even the ones I could see.
That moment when I felt the wind
Blow across my cheeks
Stinging with an arctic temperature
Even though the night was warm
I was sure my tears would freeze in place.
I think I might have even cast that wish.
Standing there under the stars and the moon
Feeling the loss of you surround me
The memory of you blanket me
The lessons learned hold me up
I wouldn't let you down
Not this time
I squared my shoulders
Put my tears away
For another day
There was work to be done
I'd make you proud
I'd earn the trust you had in me
I'd hold open hope
As I walked, the sun peaked out
From behind the hill

The Gift of Grief

The stars began to fade
I wished you could've stayed.
Ten times ten times ten more times

The Moment We'll Never Share

We'll never share that cup of coffee
Or toast life with that glass of whiskey
You'll never kiss me
Like you promised you someday would
I thought today about words spoken and unspoken
I thought today about missed opportunities
I thought today about broken connections
As I remembered when you promised
You'd come see me
Just because you'd like to
If only for one last time
Do remember that day you promised
Someday we'd be together
Even as I walked away
I was good at that
Walking away, that is
How did I get so good at staying?
Walking away felt far more natural
So the last time we talked
You spoke of visiting me
All the way out here
On the other side of the country
And I proposed we have coffee
Next time I was in your area
And I remembered that time
You whispered in my ear
That someday you'd kiss me
And I blushed with innocence
At the words as you smiled
That devilish smile
And your eyes danced with the delight
Of the tease

The Gift of Grief

But now your smile, frozen in my memory
Rests on quiet lips
Those eyes have lost all their delight
And all those promises
Of moments to connect
Have gone away with you
To a place I cannot go
But you were never the one who got away
You were simply the one who couldn't be
A reminder of all I didn't want
A remainder left over from all I wanted
A loss I never felt
Until the moment I did
I appreciate that we had the chance
To promise
A cup of coffee
A glass of whiskey
A kiss that could never be
Even though we never could see
Beyond what we never were

Remember

I remember far too much
I remember far too little
I remember your hand holding mine
I remember your tongue on my skin
I remember your arms embracing me
I remember crying on your shoulder
I remember your lips crushed against mine
I remember you listening as I talked
I remember you sharing your goals
I remember long walks on crisp, cool evenings
I remember thinking about building a future with you
I remember the leaves leaving behind summer
I remember harsh words exchanged but not the words themselves
I remember running away
I remember trying to pretend we never met
I remember forgetting the moments we shared
I remember moments sneaking back into my heart without permission
I remember a time when remembering didn't ache

Depths of My Heart

I miss you
From the depths of my heart
Where all the happy memories dance
And the sad memories entrance
I don't want to forget the good or the bad
I want to remember it all
You taught me the bad isn't always bad
And the good isn't always good
Sometimes we have to look deeper
We have to see beyond the façade
To the depths of the lives and loves we share
Where the commonalities and the differences collide
Reminding us we have so much power to unite
In ways that inspire and empower
But we also have the power to divide
In ways that destroy and dis-empower
It's our choice day after day after day
To stand up and look life and love in the eye
And ask what our next move is
And that's why every single day
I miss your smile, your presence, your wisdom
I miss you from the very depths of my heart

Falling Like Leaves

Memories falling like leaves
In shades of happy, sad, and angry
Leaving behind branches reaching
For the future filled with stars
Grounded in the roots of yesterday
Fertilizing the present with experience
Blooming into blossoms of love
Weathering the sun and the rain
Waving in the breeze
Flying away on the wind
Spreading the seeds of love far and wide
Sprouting into moments to create new memories
To fall like leaves against a bright blue sky
Where nothing hides in the life left behind
With each step forward we take
Just hold my hand as we go
And the memories falling like leaves
Won't hurt nearly so much
Because we'll face them together
The good, the bad, the indifferent
And we'll create new memories
From moments living and dying
With each passing season

Handsome Clown

Portrait of clown
Portrait of a man
Which was it?
The clown unknown
The man bleeding through
The artist's strokes of the pastel
The mischievous smile inviting mirth
The kind eyes inviting connection
The distinctive cheekbones inviting affection
The artist claimed the results were an accident
The clown never meant to represent the man
The man will live on eternally in the portrait
Telling a story that never represented the life he led.

Pain Landing

Her pain floated down
Like a leaf searching for a
A soft landing

Pathways of My Memories

Staring down the pathway to the future
Glancing back toward the pathway from the past
Standing in this present moment
Knowing there is no going back
Anticipation trails along the pathway of nerves
Covering my body making my hair stand on end
If I take one step forward, what do I leave behind?
If I stand still, can I hold on to what I lost?
Will the pathway forward be as covered with obstacles
As the path I traveled to reach this point.
You left the pathway somewhere back there
I reach back for you knowing you're but a mere memory
I cling to that memory as the pathway forward calls me
I feel your gentle push in the wind stirring the dust
My tears fall turning the dust to mud
Muddying the pathway I know I must take alone
Or at least without you
I clutch my heart as I feel your presence
Travel the neural pathways between my mind and heart
That keep you alive in me
Feel your embrace as you whisper those words I needed to hear
My future awaits down the shade dappled pathway and around the bend
I lift my leg and fear I'll lose you all over again if I put my foot down
I reach back and feel your impact on the person I've become
The one who never gives up
Set my foot down and take you with me
Because you live in all the pathways of my memories

The Villain in This Story

Is there a villain in this story?
I ask myself time and again
Seeing the pain and the loss
Feeling my own pain and loss
Is the villain the part of your body
That betrayed you?
Is the villain the medical system
That failed to fix you?
Is the villain some hidden being
That abandoned you?
Is the villain the cancer
That invaded you?
Is the villain a lack of love?
I don't know who or what
The villain in this story is
Maybe there's more than one
What I know is that my heart
Longs to defeat this villain
I can't quite find
Crawling in between the cracks
Inflicted on my heart
As I watched you disappear
Beneath a sneaky villain
Who refused to be seen
Until it was too late
To launch an attack
Allowing the villain to defeat the hero
In this story
There's no happy ending when the villain wins

Waiting Room

There was no waiting room
Waiting rooms have been closed
So we waited where we could
Knowing even as we waited
We didn't want what we waited for
As inevitable as it was
Holding our breath
Holding our tears
Holding our hearts
Waiting for what was coming
Waiting for what we couldn't stop
Knowing a waiting room wouldn't
Have made what was coming any better
So we waited
And when the waiting was done
We no longer knew what to do
So we waited some more
Hoping the inevitable just wasn't true

Last Day

The last day
We have together
Will come far too soon
Whether tomorrow or in decades
Because it's always too soon
For the last day
When you love someone
We always want
One more touch
One more hug
One more kiss
One more day
One more moment
But, someday, we will
Inevitably face
The last day

Immortality of Mortality

Thinking of your life
Lived so out loud
For all to experience
The quiet your mortal enemy
As I listen for your voice
I find it has become mine too
I close my eyes and look
For your face on my eyelids
Because I'll never see your eyes
Light up again
And the moment feels so mortal
And so immortal all at once
This pain my new companion
As I long for one more moment
Of time with you
And I know it would never be enough
Even if you could somehow be immortal
Instead of us living in this life far too mortal
Your suffering ended
And with its end I realized
The only thing truly immortal is our mortality

Moving On

Standing in the shadows
Watching you move on
Hurt more than I let on
I just couldn't tell you
Leaving would break my
World into pieces
Forget about my heart
You moving on shattered
My world in ways I still can't fathom
I knew it was best for you
You'd suffered too long
And you needed to let go
To move on
Or to stop moving
Whatever the case might be
But today when I need you most
I look to the skies
I whisper in the wind
I close my eyes and imagine
I feel a scream building in my chest
Because you can't come back
And as much as you prepared me
To be independent
I still need you
But I couldn't keep you
So I let you move on
With tears in my eyes
Even as I reassured you
I could survive without you
Because you needed to let go
And move on
There was no turning back

The Empty Chair

Across the room
Sat the empty chair
No one sat in it
No one dared
It had once been occupied
But no longer
The occupant long gone
I stared at the chair
I wanted to sit in it
But I dared not
It was your chair
It had always been
Your chair
Now it sat empty
Because you could no longer
Occupy it
I wanted to feel your presence
Once last time
I approached the empty chair
Stared at it
Touched the arm
Turned away not willing
To be the one to sully
Your last sitting place
And so your chair
Remains the empty chair
It has been since
You've no longer
Been able to sit in it

Idle Hands

Never one for idle hands
You created and built
A lifetime of memories and moments
You left behind a legacy
Of love and hard work
You handed your family
The callouses you earned
On hands never idle
Held to the very end
In love and understanding
Your hands building and rebuilding
Making the old new again
Seeing the puzzle of the broken
As a challenge to make whole again
What others couldn't see
Those hands never idle
Even to the very end
Taking care of everyone
With actions greater than words
Rest now
Let your loving, calloused hands finally be idle

Note: Also appeared on Write with TLC and Medium

Nothing Feels Regular

The regular feels irregular
On days like today
Nothing fits quite right
Seams rip in revolt
Hems fray in the mud
Waistlines drift and restrict
Nothing feels right
On days when the moon
Appears in the middle of the afternoon
While the sun shines
Darkness flirting around the edges of day
Shadows lurking in the light
So I search for the regular comforts
A cup of tea
A hot bath
A hug
An embrace
A walk with a friend
A beloved voice
A happy memory
Yet even those feel off-kilter
On days like today
As I jump from one thing
To another to make my heart stop aching
Petting my cats
Holding my love
Writing my pain
Nothing feels quite right
Nothing feels quite regular
On a day when the world
Feels like it's forgotten how to turn

This Tear Holds You

This tear holds you
And I can't wipe it away
That would be like
Giving up on you
So I hold the tear
Against my cheek
Let it dry on my skin
Feel it there each time I smile
Reminding me
You're still there
Until my skin
Absorbs the tear
Holding you
I wonder if
The next time I cry
It will be the tear
That holds you

One Last Sight

Sliding into sight
The trees below
The rooftops
The city streets
Traffic moving
I stared down
From the plane window
Seeing the state of my birth
Coming into focus
Recognizing nothing
Yet all felt familiar
Wanting to land
And wanting to fly forever
Landing brought me closer
To the reality I didn't want to see
Yet I had to face it, I had to see it
I had to see you one last time

Looking out the window
Sliding out of sight
Traffic moving
The city streets
The rooftops
The trees below
Flying away from the place
I first called home
Losing focus of what was
Flying way from the familiar
The reality I didn't want to face
Living in my broken heart forever
Having seen you one last time

Midnight

The clock strikes midnight
Another day ends silent
You are still not here

You Were Love

You were love
A little ball of love
Furry and playful
Dragging your fishy pole
All over the house
Up and down the stairs
To present for play
Your little head on my chest
Your eyes looking up into mine
Your little paw on my arm
Your little paw petting the air
Your little voice punctuating the air
Demanding I hear you
Letting me know what you wanted
Always, always, always
Exuding love from every part of your being
Encouraging me to love you as freely as you loved
You were love
And love lives on in hearts where it's cherished
And so you live on in my heart
Where you are cherished as the love you were

My Little Diva

You're gone
I stare at your blank face
Willing you to come back
Knowing you can't
It's not possible
People try to tell me
I did the right thing
Helping you go
But you didn't go
You just are no more
If you went
You could come back
But you can't
But while you were here
Oh, while you were here
You brightened every room
You demanded all the attention
Your little paw on my arm
Your tiny head against my shoulder
Your eyes looking up at me so sweetly
So much love in that tiny body
So riddled with pain
Comforting me to the end
You are forever my little diva

Heart Echoes

Your heart echoed against mine
Love bouncing off beats
Rumbling through veins
Racing for a future unknown
Tears falling against the backdrop
Of pain in another's face
Wondering what words would help
Longing to offer a comforting hug
To a stranger losing the heart
That echoed against his

You Cannot Be Found

The loss doesn't feel real
I still look for your face
In the clouds and the lakes
Determined to find you somewhere
Rather than accept
You cannot be found
Some things just can't be fixed
And I can't bring you back
To this place
No matter how much I want to
I listen for your voice
In the storm raging
Through the trees
Determined to find you somewhere
Rather than accept
You cannot be found
Yet, you are so much a part
Of my heart I just don't know how
To feel the loss of you
Even though I know that no matter
How hard I search
You cannot be found

Quiet Words

We were tumultuous
You and I
Never quite getting along
We argued
We insulted
We ignored
You thought I talked too much
I thought you were a show-off
I never admitted I admired you
Maybe I didn't know it, at least not then
You played basketball with elegance
You made friends with ease
You laughed and joked with abandon
You wore confidence like a multi-colored cloak
You teased me mercilessly
I was sure you hated me
Yet you reached out
Like none other had
When you saw behind the façade
Upon hearing words not meant for your ears
I still remember those quiet words you spoke
The look in your eyes
The expression on your face
A mix of anger, compassion, and concern
I wanted to make you understand
It wasn't as bad as it sounded
I feared you'd tell someone
I wondered if we could be friends
But then you were no more
Your charming smile
Your teasing nature
Your lanky height

Your freckles and red hair
Never knowing the maturity
I glimpsed in those few words you whispered
A teenage boy
Life cut short
Never knowing just how much
Your quiet words changed my life

Note: Also appeared on Write with TLC and Medium

City Morning, Country Morning

Morning sounds rush by me
Standing on the sidewalk
This city where people
Barely see one another
As they rush by seeking
A shot of coffee to fend
Off the sleepiness
Traffic whizzes by
Interrupting even thoughts
Emotions rise to the surface
As I remember different mornings
A gentle knock on my door
My name spoken softly but firmly
Waking up to face my day
No waiting in lines
No traffic rushing by
No standing in line for coffee
Days that will come no more
Have morphed into a new reality
Where I wake myself
Make my own coffee
Listen to the morning
And wonder which morning is better
And there's one thing I know for sure
It isn't the mourning that wakes me each morning
With a stab to the heart at your absence
So I wonder if just for old time's sake
You could knock on my door
Say my name softly but firmly
To wake me to face my day
Because your city girl misses her country daddy

TJ, More Than a Dog

Today I remembered
My tears soaking your fur
Your sparkle as we ran
Across the yard
Through the creek
Into the woods
You racing from my bicycle wreck
To the house and back
Barking like the world was ending
Until I stood and dusted myself off
Then you sniffed and licked and panted
While I hopped back on my bike and rode
I remember you holding the sucker stick between your paws
Licking and finally crunching down
Dropping the stick at my feet
Begging for another with a simple look in your eye
I remember you waiting
Day after day
As I exited the bus after school
Always on the yard side of the bridge
Anxious and happy
Tail wagging and I swear
A smile on your face
Your eyes sparkling as you searched my face
What kind of day did I have?
You always knew if I needed
You to walk quietly beside me
You to lick my hand
You to stop and let me pet you
How often I took for granted
Your desire to make things better
Your desire to celebrate good things

The Gift of Grief

Your need to protect me from danger
You were my best friend
How abandoned you must have felt
When my life changed
I went away and rarely came home
I told myself you understood
Life was better away than there
But you were still there
I knew the farm gave you joy
And I believed someday
I'd come back for you
We'd go away and live
In some special place
That was just ours
Yours and mine
I thought you'd wait for me
I never stopped to realize
Your life wouldn't last that long
My heart still aches
That I wasn't there to hold your head
To bury my face in your furry neck
To run my hand over your back
To look into your eyes
To thank you for all you gave me
So unselfishly
To say I love you
So today I cry
Because I still miss you
Because I want to a do-over
Because I want you to know
You were my best friend
Because I can never get that moment back
When you tried to jump in my car as I loaded it
When you tried to stop me from leaving

When you slunk away after I made you get out of the car
The last moment when I drove away and saw you
Sitting beside the bridge watching me go
And I wondered what you were thinking
You looked different that time
Did you know?
Were you sad?
Did you give up?
My tears flow as I remember
Because I want you know
I never wanted to get away from you
Never, ever
I only wanted a life I couldn't have
If I stayed
You were always a part of my dreams
A part of my future
A part of my goals
And then you were no more
And I felt so alone

Your Existence

You existed
I know you did
I stood in your smile
Basking in your pride
Mimicking your stride
They said I was a miniature you
And I beamed every single time
I heard those words
Even as you encouraged me
To find my own path
Watching me move away
No matter how much you
Wanted me to stay
You never tried to stop me
Even when I knew
You wanted to
The influence you had
On me and so many others
Lives on in us and every move
We make
And even when others can't see
I know you existed
Because you still exist
In my photos
In my heart
In all those little ways
That lead all those people
To call me a miniature you
As if anyone could ever be you
And now I know
Your existence mattered
Even if you didn't seem to know it

You existed and I'm
All the better for it

All the Oxygen

She sucked all the oxygen from the room
The rest of us stood there gasping to breathe.
Our pain mattered not one whit to her
As we stood there devastated.
The rest of us dissolved
In her overwhelming need to be
Center of attention.
So when we could have come together
We were all left searching for the oxygen
We needed just to stay standing.
On our own like so many times before
Seeking the oxygen she stole from us all
Even as we sought to share our oxygen with each other
And with her
Knowing if we all inhaled and exhaled together
We could get through the pain scarred but still standing
But, no, she couldn't leave any oxygen for anyone else
Why did we think this time would be any different?

Asked to Believe

You asked me to believe
In an afterlife you couldn't prove
To make my loss feel less like a loss
And more like a temporary separation
I tried to believe in what you described
But what you asked me to believe in
Sounded like hell
And I wondered why I'd want my beloved there
It seems selfish to believe in something
Just to salve my own pain
No matter how much I wanted to believe

Another Evening Comes

Morning starts my day without you
Looking for you in all your hiding places
Missing your little face looking up into mine
Afternoon sneaks up on me once again
Awaiting your presence on my chair arm
Tapping my arm with your little hand
Climbing onto my lap
Front legs on my desk, back legs on my legs
Realizing once again you can't come to me
Another evening comes
And I look for you once again
Your dinner spot as empty as it was at breakfast
I almost call for you, catch myself at the last moment
Another evening comes
Sitting on the couch, positioning the covers
Waiting for you to come and settle in
Waiting and waiting and waiting
Until my heart aches again with your absence
Snuggling under the covers
Issuing my goodnights
Your goodnight catches in my throat
Or maybe it's in my tears as I blink them back
I miss our routines
Our morning routine
Our afternoon routine
Our evening routine
But then I close my eyes and dream
You back into life

Echoing

I listen for your little voice
Always so demonstrative
So many different meows
Echoing through my home
Letting me know
You were happy
You were mad
You wanted my attention
You were in pain
You were hungry
Each sound slightly different
Even a different one as response to
Each of our names
Expressing your opinions
Demanding your needs
Echoing through my home
Communicating as best you could
Even when I didn't quite understand
I close my eyes and listen
But I no longer hear your meow
Echoing through my house
So I listen to my heart
And there it is
Where it can never be silenced
Echoing through my heart

Weep, Keep, Sleep

Left alone to weep
Your heart no longer to keep
I lost you in sleep

Appointments

Some things can't be scheduled
Or even if they are
Come as a shock to the system
No matter how well planned for
Looking into the eyes of a loved one
Losing life reminds us
That some appointments
Can't be skipped
Can't be scheduled
Can't be procrastinated
No matter how much we want to avoid them
As we stare into the eyes of an appointment
We never wanted to have
How do we cling to the memories that came before
When all we can see is the appointment breaking our hearts?

Are You Ready?

You asked if I was ready
Ready for what was all I could respond
You raised an eyebrow and said I knew what
But I didn't
How could I be ready?
So much had changed
I still couldn't read your mind
Wasn't sure I wanted to
Was sure I didn't want you to read mine
So was I ready
Did it matter
The time arrived
Whether I was ready or not
I steeled myself for the moment at hand
And watched you slip away
Even though you'd been gone
For so long it felt like
I'd been losing you for years
Ever since you shared the news
I could never be ready to hear
And then you were gone
And I knew I wasn't ready
I would never be ready
Even though you were ready
To let go so the pain would end
I'm still not ready…

Last Breath

The wind kissed my chapped lips
Burning as I tried not to smile
The thought on my mind
Bringing you closer than
You could possibly be
Saying goodbye crushed me
In all the ways I couldn't dare say
Watching you in such distress
Ripped asunder by need to keep you
From your need to find peace
My selfish heart still decries
The day you took your last breath
Seeing you so lifeless
Drained the life right out of me
Knowing your suffering was no more
Should have brought me some relief
Yet I stood there feeling more lost
Than I'd ever felt in my life
Finding my way now
Leaves me feeling more alone
Than I've ever felt in my life
Just yesterday I blinked back tears
As I remembered little moments
That seemed so insignificant and realized
There are so many more I've forgotten
I wondered once again if the emptiness you left
Will ever be filled
Even as I know it can't possibly be
It's the empty spot left by you
And no one can ever take your place

April of Grief

It isn't the mourning that wakes me each morning
In a heart that longs for just one moment
Seeing the puzzle of the broken
Reverberating through my grief
In search of the nature all around me
To make my loss feel less like a loss

Does my love create anti-love?
Subtracting you from my life zeroed out my heart
Leaving my life to change in ways I can't yet imagine
Yet, every time I feel my unhealed heart split open
I knew I had to let you go
Because the heart loves beyond the loss

Echoing through my heart
Where you'll live until I take my last breath
Still trying to comfort me even as I comforted you
The kind eyes inviting connection
Until the very last moment
Riding on a wave we can't control

Nostalgia so great we lost our voice
Looking into the eyes of a loved one
Ripping love from our lives
Now it's our job to carry on your legacy
To live all the stories of our lives
So our lives will mean something

Looking into the storm of grief
Crawling in between the cracks
An embrace bigger than life
In the hearts left behind

We didn't want what we waited for
And love lives on in hearts where it's cherished

Let go of your last breath
Then I begged my tears to come back, too

Saying Goodbye

She tied a red bow
Around his lean finger
Watched him park the truck
Next to the saw he'd never use again
She wanted to tear the ribbon to shreds
Instead, she wound her fingers around his and waited
The wound he would leave would never disappear
Her tears would have to wait though
If he saw them, it would break his heart
She needed a walk in the park
And someone besides him to lean on
As he took his final bow

Get Back Here

I looked into your lifeless eyes
My heart screamed
"Get back here! Get back here right now!"
I touched you and knew
I wasn't ready
I would never be ready
No matter how ready I thought I was
No matter how I knew it was the best thing for you
My heart, my mind, my selfishness screamed
"Get back here! Get back here right now!"
Tears filled my eyes and spilled all over the place
I cried and cried and cried
Until I'm sure I ran out of tears
Then I begged my tears to come back too
Because they had somehow become my link to you
My heart aches with the loss even as I remember
Every moment we shared
How you suffered in those final days
How I wanted to take your suffering away at any cost
Even at the cost of never getting you back
And, still, I whisper to the sun, the stars, the sky
"Get back here! Get back here right now!"
Maybe someday I'll stop but for now
I cry to the rain, the wind, the moon
Please deliver my message
"Get back here! Get back here right now!"

How Can Goodbye Be Good?

I told you goodbye
For the last time
And even then I couldn't
Say the word.
How can this parting be good?
How can losing you be good?
How can goodbye be good?
I didn't want to let you go
As selfish as keeping you would've been
So I played with the words
To pretend this permanence was temporary
I wanted to believe I'd wake up tomorrow
And there you'd be smiling at me once again
Then I remembered tomorrow never comes
And this goodbye is far too final…

Wind Carries Your Whisper

The wind carries your whisper
That quiet voice you held at the end
When it seemed every word you said
Was part of a great secret we shared
So unlike the voice I remembered
Which was never exactly loud
But held a confidence I mimicked as a child
And learned to hold when mine failed as a young woman
I wanted to be you
Moving through the world with strength and courage
You were the bravest man I knew
Until the very end
When your voice began to falter
And my heart ached as you expressed the words
Built up in your heart filled with love
That moment when I held your hand to comfort you
As you'd held mine so many times to comfort me
And felt you squeeze mine back as my eyes teared up
Still trying to comfort me even as I comforted you
Strong and steady as the wind blowing through my window
You left me with that

Hold Your Grief

Tell me all there is to say
Don't hold back a single sound
Let me hear your grief, your pain, your need
Spill the words like red wine on white cotton
Let me hold your memories when they get too heavy
Let me hold you above water when you forget to swim
Let me hold your hand when you feel all alone
Let me hold you when you need a soft place to land
I'll cherish your truth imprinted on my heart
So you can find your joy again
Until the next time grief floods your heart
And leaves you grasping the loss
Intensified by the memories
That make you smile as much as they make you weep

The First Tear

A tear welled in the corner of my eyes
I knew if it slid down my cheek
A waterfall would follow
I held it at bay
I refused to let it fall
Feared a million more would follow
Then a shock hit
An unexpected blow
Forcing that first tear
To fall from a heart
Shattered into a million pieces
A piece for each tear
The pain finally overwhelmed the control
And those tears fell
Clouding the past and the present
Overwhelming the future
A loss followed by another
Looking into the storm of grief
Compounding as life stepped forward
Leaving me standing in its wake
Trying not to drown in my tears
Until I wondered if I had any tears left
Wishing I'd somehow been able to stop
The one that started them all
And yet feeling absolutely relieved
To finally release the first tear

We're Not Dancing Anymore

Your feet stumbled over mine
I slowed down and let you lead
But you stumbled again
This time I held you up
Until you found your footing
Eventually we found a rhythm
Or something resembling a rhythm
It matched nothing I could remember
Ever dancing before, but I gave you my all
We danced to the rhythm you set
For so long I forgot there could be another rhythm
Then suddenly it all changed
We stood still, staring at one another and wondered
What happened as
You disappeared from my embrace.
All I could think was
We're not dancing anymore
Come back, I miss your broken rhythm

Haunted Heart

The ghost of your love
Haunts my heart
Hiding in corners
Barely a whisper
That refuses to be quiet
A poltergeist knocking
Against the doors
A wraith peeking
Out the windows
A phantom pacing
The halls
What spell can I cast
What charm can I wear
What potion can I make
What protection can I conjure
To drive this haunting out
No, don't tell me
I'm not sure I'm ready to hear
What if it works?
I'd lose this tenuous connection to you
Sometimes I wonder if I really want
To stop being haunted by
The ghost of your love

Heart Stop

If my heart should stop
Without saying what needs said
Will the words still breathe

Prime Beliefs

You primed me to believe
We would have infinity
You would be here forever
So when your days were numbered
Countdown to three two one

I reached into my mathematical formulas
To prime my beliefs that days could multiply
I tried to find a way to make three two one
Turn into ninety-seven and then one more
Time after time

I looked for the heavens that would keep you
Living for my benefit making you shine in the stars
Seeking to find the square root of love
Hiding in the prime numbers I didn't want to divide
Subtracting you from my life zeroed out my heart

You primed me to believe infinity was possible
So I clung to my prime belief we would have forever

The Weight of Love

Today love feels like
A weight on my heart
Weighing me down
Pulling me under
Until I just might drown
It presses against the past
And longs for the future
Anything to escape this moment
Where the heaviness hurts
Love presses against the sadness
Coming from circumstances I cannot control
It might seem like I don't feel the weight
Because I don't burden you with my grief
But know I feel the heaviness of love
When pain invades loved one's lives
Leaving a muddy, rocky path ahead
Your loss might not be my loss
But my love for you becomes heavy
In your moment of pain
But I won't let go
I'll hold on tight
Keep my head above the fray
Because someday, someday
Love will again feel light

Beyond My Reach

My eyes shot open
The room was still dark
Yet I was sure a light shone
Somewhere just beyond my reach
I reached out
Tears streaming down my face
I can't reach you
I can't reach you
I can't reach you
Try as I might
This world refuses to bend to my will
Giving me hope that today will bring
The answer I can't have
So I dry my tears
Turn from the light I cannot see
Close my eyes
Reach into my heart
Where I can still reach you
Feel you with me as I tell myself a story
A story to pretend just so I can get through the night
Tomorrow will come again
And I still won't be able to reach you.
Until I can
My heart will reach for you

Convicted by Death

I listened for your voice
Knowing your words would be great
If only you could find a part to play
Finding reasons to love the Spring season
Even if it meant you had to find a way to convict
The past for losing a hard run race

You promised me you didn't judge by life's race
In a loudly whispered hoarse voice
But I couldn't find a way to pardon the convict
Even though you promised she was great
When you last saw her in the Fall season
Of the rewrite of your last play

But as I watched her baby play
I knew the child couldn't run the race
Winter somehow became the hottest season
The baby's cries attempting to voice
The divide between us grown so great
Nothing could undo the pain of the convict

When in the end the casket imprisons the convict
The music ceases to play
Notes that have fallen silent no matter how great
Little feet have long since ceased to race
Toward the much beloved now silenced voice
Because summer has become the darkest season

Searching for the light of a new season
To release the convict
Into the wind carrying the lost voice
Calling us all to come play

Watching the past race
Toward a future we hope will be great

Remembering moments with smiles so great
That spanned season after season after season
Running each in our own race
Never expecting death to convict
Us in the midst of our play
As if we had no voice

Nostalgia so great we lost our voice
Stumbled in our race to avoid becoming the convict
As the final season brought an end to our play.

Inconvenience

Sometimes I wonder
Would your heart ache if I died?
Would you shed a single tear?
Would you just be annoyed by the inconvenience?
What would you do with
All the things that represent me?
You have such disdain for them now while I'm alive
Too much inconvenience in your life
Would you suddenly develop
An unbreakable attachment
To the thing that most
Represents me to you?
What would that thing even be?
Or would you just toss it all
In the trash without a second thought?
Disposing of me as easily as a broken glass
Every trace of my existence erased
From your life
Annoyed by the inconvenience I am once again
Because I won't be here
To clean up that mess for you

Someday Satchel

I packed all those unwanted emotions
In a satchel and secured it
Promising myself I'd get back to them
At a more appropriate time
I told myself I needed a safe place
To express them
But where is that safe place?
I can't seem to find it.
I look at the satchel from time to time
Even play with the latch securing it
Knowing someday I'll have to open it
Feel all those emotions I don't want to feel
Face all those moments I packed away for another day
But, for now, my satchel awaits me, tucked away in the corner
Only opened on occasion to quickly stuff in the next thing
Closed again before the previous things can get out
Because I must keep my head up, square my shoulders, and
Soldier on
Even as the satchel bulges to the point of pulsing
With everything that needs released
Maybe someday I whisper as I pat it day after day
Maybe someday

I'm Here

You handed me flowers
To express your sympathy
I accepted with a thank you
We'd met the expectations
Both showed how thoughtful we were
But it was what came next that
Was truly thoughtful
You pushed the flowers aside
Took my hand in yours
Looked into my eyes
Said simply "I'm here"
I nodded and smiled
Through the tears I blinked back
Staring at me, you said quietly
Your voice barely a whisper
"I'm here. You don't have to be brave."
I nodded again, speechless
"Not with me. Let it go."
The tears slipped from my eyes
Slid down my cheeks
Little did you know the courage it took
To let those tears flow
But, you, oh you
You knew just how to touch
The part of me that needed to release
All the grief inside
Your presence in that moment
Was the most thoughtful thing I'd ever seen
As you held me and my tears with tenderness
Finally, I was safe to grieve

Changing the Bed

This morning I stripped the sheets
From the mattress
Ripping away the last of your scent
Feeling your essence slip away
Into the dust bunnies rising up
The window let in the sunshine
The sun felt like you smiling on my skin
As I felt the darkness in my heart lighten
I remembered the last time you touched me
Your lips lingering on mine with longing
As you slipped away from me
I dropped the sheets to the floor
Sank beside them refusing to give way
To the tears building behind my eyes
You won't be back
Not this time
I looked at the bed
The mattress cold and sterile
The headboard and footboard dark with age
Does it remember you like I do?
I shoved the mattress off its rails
It fell against the wall
Mocking me with the stain of yesterday
I released the footboard
It fell to the floor with a thud
Cracked like the sweet, secret words we last spoke
I released the headboard
It fell forward against the frame
Leaning there like my love for you
I picked up the sheets
Carried them to the washer
Thought again

The Gift of Grief

Turned to the trash
Let them fall there
Letting you go
A shiver went up my spine
As I closed the door on the past
Your love wrapped around me like a blanket
That won't ever fray at the edges
This morning I changed our bed for the last time
Tomorrow I'll make mine for the first time

Seeking Closure

After the mourning
Broke into a new beginning
Creating a guilty heart
Dependent on memories
Everlasting memories
For the comfort of forgetting
Guilty hearts can move forward
Hearing only yesterday's song
In the rhythm of lost anchors
Jostling for first place
Kicking the heart into recess
Moving only enough to breathe
Nostalgia through the veins
Opening closed eyes
Purposefully refusing to see today
Quietly give way to yesterday
Refusing a future filled with possibility
Stalled by the grief of denial
Taunting the truth with deception
Underneath all the brilliant smiles
Vacating reality in favor of fantasy
Where mourning is unnecessary
Xylophones play happy songs
Yesterday comforts the soul
Zen arrives with the moon's rise

To Cry About

Nothing left to cry about
I uttered the words
Meaning them yet not
Feeling them deeply
Expressing them shallowly
Casually offering them
As if they'd change something
Looking back I see the desperation
Of needing a reason to cry
And feeling like even that was gone
In the moment of despair
Overwhelming my dry eyes
Wondering if I'd ever cry again
Because everything that mattered
Was already nothing more than dust
So I looked around at those who
Waited for my tears to fall
Refusing to give them the satisfaction
Waiting until I sat alone
In a dark room feeling all the tears
My heart hoarded against the pain
I couldn't allow myself to feel
As I proclaimed for anyone
Who would listen
I have nothing left to cry about
Little did they know it was because
I knew that tears wouldn't help
Because there was nothing left
This last heartbreak
Was the one no one could fix
So with that knowledge
I lost all my reasons

To cry the tears that
Refused to stop flowing
From eyes betraying me

Clinging Thoughts

Am I clinging to these thoughts?
Or
Are they clinging to me?
I think about you
Looking at me
The way you always did
I miss that
I hold on to the memory of it
Even though the thought of it hurts
Hurts like hell right now
Because it also comforts me
Comforts me like heaven right now
When I think about never seeing
You look at me that way again
I feel lost, abandoned, adrift
When I think about every time
You looked at me
I feel so lucky, grateful, grounded
And all these feeling are all mixed up
In a heart that longs for just one more moment
With you
Even though that heart also knows
That moment wouldn't be for you
What it would for me
Because I cling to thoughts of before
The suffering began
Because that's how I want to remember you
Today, tomorrow, yesterday
No longer matter to the thoughts
Clinging to my heart

Left This World

You left this world
A little better than you found it
You brought smiles to lips
You brought joy to hearts
You pushed us to be our best
By always doing your best
When your best failed
You stood up and tried again
Until your best won in the end
Fighting until the last moment
To make sure your presence
In this world
Made it just a little better than it had been
Now it's our job to carry on your legacy
And leave this world
Just a little better than we found it
Just like you did

Forming Love

The tears took form
Welling in the corner
Between history and future
The memories and the moments
Taking up residence
In my heart
Where they form the love
That gives me the foundation
For the life I want to live
Concrete and rebar
Boards and paint
Windows and doors
Quiet moments and parties
The laughter and tears weaving together
To form this life I inhabit
Trying to find a way to love
Even when hate is easier to find
Reaching for you in the dark
When my heart breaks into love
Knowing you can't reach back

Me Me Me
(for Meme)

Your tiny face looked up
Introducing you not by name
But by attitude
You would not be forgotten
A week later you reminded us
You belonged in our home
And then you introduced yourself
To the kitten in my arms
Claimed him in your charming way
And home with us you both came.
This was your home
On naughty days and nice days
Your cute face looking up
Reintroducing yourself every time
Making sure we never forgot you
Knew who you were and what you wanted
Always letting us know you chose us
Until the very last moment
When we had to let you go
I hope you never regretted your choice
We did our best to make your life
As wonderful as you made ours
Every time you looked up and said
Me me me…

Note: Also appeared on Write with TLC and Medium

Story of Todd

Sleeping quietly
All the others scampering
Can't take my eyes off
Your little white and gray body
Snuggled up against the edge
I wait for you to wake up
Keep glancing back
Finally, I can't wait any longer
I pick you up
Your brilliant blue eyes
Capture my heart
In less than a beat
You yawn
Not scared
Not too excited
Not agitated
Settle in
Home
Bringing you home
You bounce through the house
With such enthusiasm
Snuggles and pets
Kneads and kisses
Purring so much and so loud
Always so happy
Yet so very sensitive
To noise
To upheaval
To chaos
You loved hard
You played hard
You lived hard

Always looking for a new challenge
Entertaining yourself and us
You were life personified

Tenacious to the very end
Loving to the very end
Filling our hearts day after day
Beyond the very end
That was the story of you

Note: Also appeared on Write with TLC and Medium

Lucky Me

Today I looked at your picture
Felt lucky you'd graced my life
With your presence
Felt that familiar tug at my mouth
Followed by the familiar tug of my heart
Followed by the familiar tug of a teardrop
All mixed up together
Because you bring both the joy and the pain
As I remember your sweet face
Looking into mine
Yet, every time I feel my unhealed heart split open
I can't help but feel so incredibly lucky
You chose me to love you for your whole short life
And hope you felt just as lucky to have me love you

My Three Cats

I claim you time after time
But I never owned you
You grace me with your presence
You love me with your purrs
You calm me with your grace
You knitted a fortress around my heart
Holding together the scattered and scarred bits
I thought I'd lost
I felt you slowly take ownership
Of me
As my heart slowly healed day by day
And then there were two of you
Those of us left rudderless
Those of us left anchorless
Those of us left searching
Even as my heart held all three of you
Because the heart loves beyond the loss
Because the heart doesn't subtract
Because the heart expands
You will always be my three cats
Whether you're by my side
Or only in my memories
You'll forever be in my heart
You'll forever be my heart
Along with all the others who
Have taken up residence in my heart

Moment of Change

Life can change in a moment
Without warning
Without compassion
Without understanding
The timing of this change or that change
Never seems to be the right time
Yet, they come and come and come
Bringing love into our lives
Ripping love from our lives
Little loves and big loves
I had no idea how much losing you
Would change my life
In a moment beyond my control
You were there
Then you weren't
And there was nothing I could do
To bring you back
No matter how much my heart ached
At how your absence would change my life

Cat Hugs

Blue eyes
Slow close, slow open
Offering love
As deep as the ocean
As wide as the sky
As clear as a lake
Staring deep into mine
As I return the slow blink
Front paws sliding
To either side of my neck
Nose nuzzled into my clavicle
Reaching out from that safe place
To invite another cat in
Capturing me in that moment
How many times over the years
Would you repeat those moves?
Every time winning my heart all over again
Capturing me totally
Claiming me
Even when you could no longer quite reach

Sorry 'Bout Your Luck

Some days life hurts
Some days life heals
Some days it does both
Riding on a wave we can't control
Is it beyond our luck to know
When it will work to our advantage
And when it will break us down
When we will be lucky
When we will be unlucky
Some days when you look in the mirror
All you can say is
Sorry 'bout your luck
Then stare your luck in the face
Grab your memories and your love
Stand in the face of the pain life dealt
And tell life
Sorry 'bout your luck
Today I'm going to cherish every moment
Even the ones filled with the loss
That can never be filled
Because
To hurt is to heal
To heal is to hurt
To live is to love
To love is to live
And we still have all the memories
You left us to share and build on
As we hurt
As we heal
As we love
As we live
And that doesn't require any luck at all

Sundays and Holidays

Sundays around your
Table felt like holidays
Rippling lakes of love

My Sweet Furry Valentine

Sweet from day one
You felt like my
Furry valentine every day
And twice on Friday
Or Monday or Wednesday
It never mattered what day
I could count on you
To be loving and sweet
To seek out peace and purrs
On my lap or sitting next to me
Or even on your own
And yet you'd attack your toys
With glee and determination
So strong and sweet
Blessing my life
With your presence
The perfect valentine
Any day of the week

Stop the Changes

Life changes every minute
Whether we want it to or not
Leaving us standing still
Or dragging us along.
Watching you change
Made me long for time to stand still
To stop the changes ripping you from me
I longed to change the changes I had
No power to change
All those changes left my heart begging
For one more day, one more hour, one more second
Even as you had to change beyond my reach
Leaving my life to change in ways I can't yet imagine
All these changes beyond our control
Breaking my heart

Unplugged My Heart

I unplugged my heart
Convinced I could stop feeling
This pain would somehow stop
All the grief living there
Would dissipate
And I'd find my way back
To the moment I wanted to redo
So I could change the unchangeable
I thought if I unplugged my heart
I could shut off all the emotions
I didn't want to feel
Maybe then I'd be able
To forget what I didn't want to remember
What no one told me
Before I unplugged my heart
Was the good goes with the bad
When you shut off your heart
But even more importantly
The emotions keep coming no matter
How much you pretend you've
Unplugged your heart

Get My Heart

I miss the way
You climbed on my lap
Kneaded my legs
Settled in
Wrapped yourself around me
You little paws pointing forward
Like you just might take flight
Your blue eyes staring up at me
Slow blink times one
Times two
Movement catching your attention
Jumping down to join in the play
Looking back just for a second
Knowing just how to
Get my heart
Remembering you then
And how you lost
So much of that playfulness
But never ever lost the ability to
Get my heart
When you climbed on my lap and
Settled in even on your worst days
Blue eyes still staring up at me
Slow blink a little slower to come
Clinging a little harder to me
Instead of jumping down to play
But still glancing my way before
Drifting into a nap
As I sat and remembered…
And wondered if you dreamed…
Because baby boy
You still knew just how to

The Gift of Grief

Get my heart
And you've still got it

Unasked Answered Question

The question teased my lips
Flirted with my tongue
Slipped from my eyes
I wanted to ask you
But I wasn't sure
I could handle the answer
So I didn't ask
Instead I looked in your eyes
As your thoughts slipped away
I still saw the love there
I knew in my heart
The answer I didn't want to hear
As I hid the question in my heart
I watched your face
Your eyes answered my question
The question I couldn't put into words
I nodded quietly
I whispered that I understood
I whispered that I'd be okay
I whispered my love for you
And then as the question escaped
In tears I could no longer control
Even though I never said the words
I knew I had to let you go
Anything else would only be selfishness
So I whispered
I love you
        I love you
                I love you
Until I knew you could no longer hear
What I most wanted you to know

Your Love Lives On

You might be gone
But the love you gave
Lives on
In the hearts left behind
In the memories created
In the impact of your life
You gave it all
Setting a high bar
For all the others who followed
Sometimes your love was gentle
Sometimes your love was tough
Sometimes your love was loud
Sometimes your love was quiet
But it was always love
There was no mistaking your love
For your family
For your friends
For your community
For me
And I will share that love forward
In the love I share
Whether it be gentle, tough, loud, or quiet

Leapt

You leapt into my life
Quite by surprise
But without even a leap
The years leaped by
As you leaped through my house
Playing and loving
Sweet as could be
Leaping so high you scared me
Then one day you stopped leaping
And I knew something was wrong
Watched you for a single leap
Longed for you to leap
Reveled in the rare leap
You made short as it might be
Looked for signs your leaps
Would return
Until the day my heart leapt
As you slipped away
Right out of my life
Right out of life itself

Overdrive

Sitting calmly in the wind
The world passing us by
We chatted about the future
We lamented the past
We held the present tight
You reached for my hand
I blinked back a tear
Knowing you couldn't stay
No matter how tightly I held on
Nothing seemed to matter
In that moment but holding on
To the present
Anchoring you to my heart
Where I could hold you forever
Knowing forever wasn't real
My heart thumping in the unsaid
My tongue stumbling to form
The words you needed to hear
The words I needed you to hear
Instead we smiled
You cracked a joke
We laughed about some absurdity
The words remained unsaid
But you squeezed my hand
And I knew you knew
I knew you knew that I knew
The interruption of that moment
Sent us into overdrive
Frantic to savor every moment
We could save for memories
To keep us all tethered to you
As it became increasingly clear

Going into overdrive
Wouldn't save you
We calmed down
Enjoyed the moment
Reminisced about the past
Promised a future we wouldn't share
Watched the sun go down
And come up again
Waiting for the inevitable
Assured ourselves we were ready
We sat calmly in the stale air
Cried at denying you the wind on your face
Watched as you left us bit by bit
Pushing us into overdrive again
But you were finally calm
No longer in overdrive
To comfort all of us
Through your pain
Our hearts broke
Sending our love
Into overdrive
To keep you
Alive in our hearts

Your Scent is Gone

Close my eyes
Inhale deeply
Try to find your scent
Somewhere in the air
Hoping you left
Just a whiff of it behind
The scent I remember so fondly
But took for granted for so long
I exhale my disappointment
Try once again
Inhaling until it hurts
Holding my breath
Searching every drop of air
For your scent
Finally, I'm forced to exhale
Convincing myself there's still
A hint of you left behind
In the air I breathe
Because then you're not really gone
Someday I'll accept reality
But for today I'll inhale
Searching for your scent
One last time

The Littlest Reminder

The littlest reminder
Your voice quieted now
No longer able to speak to me
A sound I'll never hear again
Lost to the ages
Where did it go?
Did it leave even before you did?
Lost in the disease that took
So much of what you were
And took you too
The pain of yesterday still sparks
From time to time
The littlest reminder
In the grin of another
Leaving me with an equation
That I just can't solve
The one that reminds me
Sometimes the formula
Just refuses to work the way I want
And then I remember
You smiling at me
Your voice reminding me
Who I am
Time and again
As only you could
And I wonder
Has my memory rewritten
The sound of your voice
I like to think not but
I'm just not sure
As I search for

The littlest reminder
Everywhere I can

Because You Were Here

I wake up missing you
Yet again
Knowing you'll never
Return
And I remember your
Smile
I remember that one time you
Cried
I remember your
Voice
Those words I so needed to
Hear
And my heart aches
Just for a moment
As I smile remembering
All those little moments
Living in my heart
Then I blink back a tear
Remembering
All those little moments
You'll never experience
But, I am a better person
Because you were here
I look into the night sky
Try to imagine
Your absence getting easier
And I remind myself
This void only exists
Because you were here
And while you might be gone
This world is a better place
Because you were here

The Gift of Grief

And I will never forget
Your impact
No matter who else does
Because no matter what
Else is lost
I still feel you in my heart
Because you were here
And no one can take that away
I realized today this pain, this grief
Is worth it even if it never ends
Because you were once here

You Are the Sky

Last night I looked up at the sky
The stars your eyes twinkling
The clouds filled with your unshed tears
The moon the tilt of your head
The wind your voice rising above the noise
I opened my arms
Felt you surround me
An embrace bigger than life
The sky hugging me as tightly as you always did
That's when I knew
You might be gone but
You are the sky forevermore

Release You

Whisper in my ear
Tell me it'll all be okay
I won't believe you
But I need to hear you
Tickle my neck
With your warm breath
Reassuring me you're still here
Even when you're not
Because I need to feel you
Hold me tight against you
When my world falls apart
Holding me together
When you can't be found
Because I need to lean on you
Let me inhale all of you
In the air around me
When I can't catch a breath
Because I need to smell you
Let me see your smile
In the clouds
One last time
As you evaporate from my life
Because I don't ever want to forget you
Dry this tear I can't hold back
Kiss my cheek as only you can
When I fall to the ground
Because nothing matters anymore
I can't let go of you
Please don't make me
Face this life without you
I'm not sure what's left
Hiding in the hole you dug in my life

As you slipped into oblivion
Leaving me in the wake
Of an ocean rising ever faster
I can't swim fast enough
To outrun this pain
The air has grown thinner
As I gasped trying to hold you near
I reached for you and found me
Your words whispering in the stars
Written on the moon
Traipsing across the mountains
Living in my heart
Pumping through my veins
I look up
I look down
I look around me
I release you
            I release you
                      I release you
Thank you

Tasting Memories

I tasted the rain
As it landed on my tongue
One drop then another
Mingling with the taste of
The forest around me
My first inkling taste
Lingers in the air
Reminding me that
The tastes we hold
In our memories
Connect us to each other
Holding us with honesty
As we deceive ourselves
Into believing this taste
Is something more than it is
Do you remember the tastes
Of the most important moments
Of the most painful moments
Of the most beautiful moments
Of all the places you've ever been
Of all the moments you've ever lived
Of all the experiences you've ever lost
The taste of the rain reminded me
Of the taste of straw as Daddy cut hay
And I found myself looking for the
Taste of the sun in a cloudy day
Encouraging me to taste the air
To see if I could taste the rainbow
Hugging the sky
But all I could taste in that moment
Was the lingering longing for
All those tastes lost along the way

The Gift of Grief

Grief brings you back to me
In the moments when I
Need you the most
The habit of you holds my hand
As my tears fall in moving forward
Without you by my side
A smile alights my face
A moment before tears
Fill my eyes
And I remember you comforting me
Even through your own pain
And the grief overwhelms
For just a moment
Then it reminds me
You were really here
Brightening my day
Just by your mere existence
Even when you tried my patience
Your imperfections making you all the more
Perfect in my eyes
Whenever something reminds me
You are gone
Never to return
My heart reminds me you live on
In my memories
In all you taught me
In the life I live
In the love I give
And in that moment
Like so many others
Grief brings you back to me

The Gift of Grief

Acknowledgments

My thanks to Loay Abu-Husein for helping me turn my idea for the cover into a workable cover.

Thanks to Kate Allen and Lori Felmey for their feedback on the cover as it was in development.

Thank you to all the friends and family who have read my work, encouraged me to keep writing, and inspired me along my journey.

Other Books By T. L. Cooper

Poetry:

Democracy in Silhouette

Vulnerability in Silhouette

Strength in Silhouette

Memory in Silhouette

Reflections in Silhouette

Love in Silhouette

Short Stories:

Take a Chance & Other Stories of Starting Over

Soaring Betrayal

Fiction:

All She Ever Wanted

About the Author

T. L. Cooper is the author of two collections of short stories, several books of poetry, and a novel. Her poems, short stories, articles, and essays have appeared online, in books, and in magazines. She grew up on a farm in Tollesboro, Kentucky. She now lives in Albany, Oregon. When not writing, she enjoys yoga, golf, hiking, creating plant-based recipes, and traveling.

www.ingramcontent.com/pod-product-compliance
Lightning Source LLC
Chambersburg PA
CBHW051807040426
42446CB00007B/564